THE HISTORY OF BIESEMEYER BOATS
by Bill Biesemeyer
2010

This history book was made for my two children, my nine grandchildren and my twenty-six great-grandchildren. It would not have come about without my brother, Rusty, who designed the best flatbottom sprint boat, Julian Pettengill, the greatest driver of Biesemeyer Boats, and many hours of dedicated work on the computer by my daughter, Diane Palmer.

The First Biesemeyer Boats - 1949

In 1946, I was 19 years old and had just finished two years in the Navy. I went to work for George Mishey in Phoenix, Arizona building outboard hydroplanes. At that time, outboard hydroplane racing was very popular.

After that, I worked in cabinet shops for a while. I was always good at working with wood.

In 1949, I built my first boat in a tin shed in the back of Baldy Davison's motorcycle shop. It was a 9-foot, 3-point hydroplane.

I had been going to boat races with Mishey and knew a lot of the boat racers. One of them was a man named Elgin Gates from Needles, California who had a boat business and also raced boats. I called Elgin, told him that I had just built a 3-point hydroplane, and asked him if he would be interested in buying one. Elgin said to bring it over.

I got my brother, Rusty, to go with me to Needles with the boat tied to the top of Rusty's car. Elgin liked it. Elgin put a motor on it then he, Rusty, and I went down to the river to try it out. After Elgin was out for a while, he came back to shore and said, "I'll take it, Bill, and you can build me another one." He paid $350 for each boat. My boats were made out of fir and pine so they were less expensive but they performed really well. This was the start of Biesemeyer Boats.

> A hydroplane is a type of boat used for racing. A three point hydroplane has two flat surfaces forward and one in the back. The forward points (sponsons) are lower than, and are outboard of, the main hull. The third point is the back end of the boat.
>
> Prior to the 1950s, boats were a product made almost exclusively of wood. Fiberglass was still a rather exotic material which didn't find its way into the mainstream of boat-building until a few years later. That meant boats were still handcrafted, one at a time, by incredibly skilled finish carpenters.

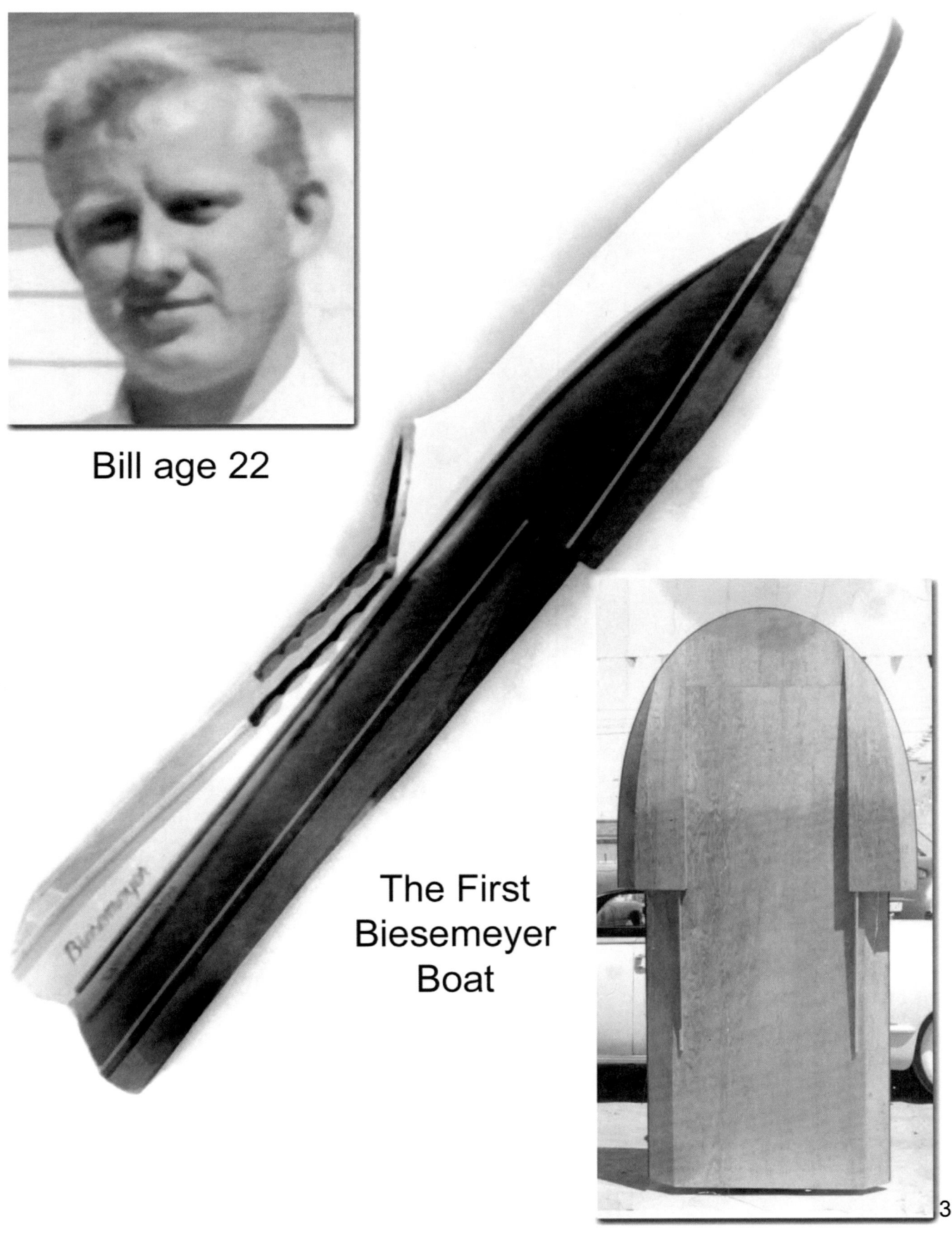

Bill age 22

The First Biesemeyer Boat

Arizona Boat Works 1956
The First Biesemeyer Ski Boats

I didn't build any other boats until 1956 when Rusty became very interested in boats. He went to a retired man named Milton Edgar and borrowed money to start a boat company to build ski boats. Rusty and I started Arizona Boat Works in early 1956 and built the first Biesemeyer ski boats.

Our business was at 1009 W. Taylor in Phoenix. The boats were built out of pine and fir with bolted-in steel rails for installing the engine. We built six boats and they really performed well.

I built the wooden hulls and Rusty put fiberglass coverings on the outside and painted them. We only installed engines on three of the boats and the customers installed the engines on the other three. One of the boats had a direct-drive Studebaker engine and the other two had small Chevy engines that were set up with V-drives.

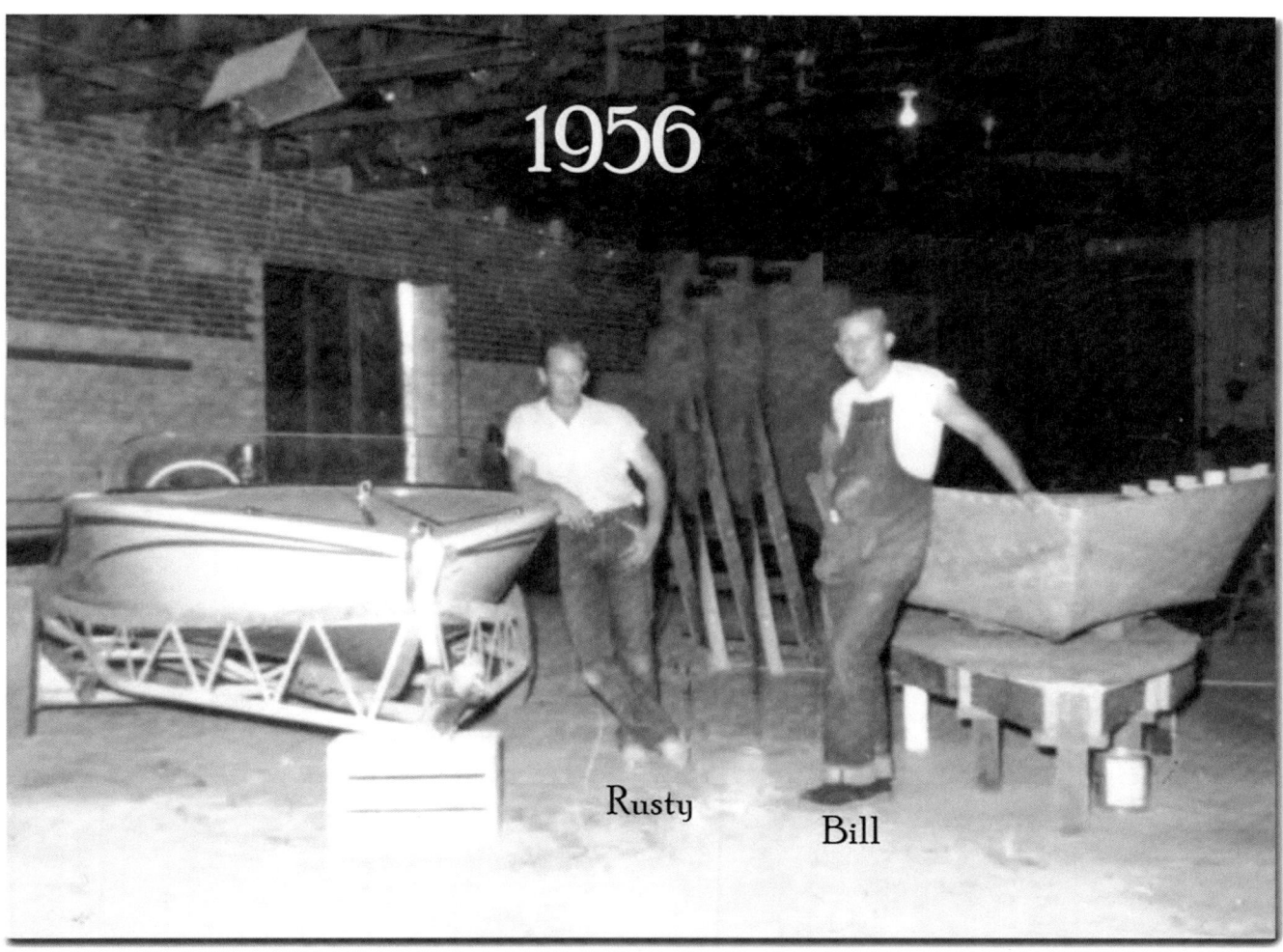

1956

Rusty   Bill

Phoenix Brothers Open Boat Works

Two Phoenix brothers, students of pleasure boat styling for 10 years, have opened the Arizona Boat Works at 1009 W. Taylor.

They are Rusty and William Biesemeyer, both of whom have been employed by other Valley boat-building firms.

The brothers said that in four months they have produced three pilot models — 16-foot, water-ski crafts with 60 horsepower motors. Rusty says that they are now setting up a production method whereby 8 to 10 of the plywood, fiber glass coated boats can be made every month.

The brothers believe that hull design of their boats makes them especially suitable for use on Arizona lakes by water-ski enthusiasts.

The Arizona Republic   Thursday, August 9, 1956

RUSTY BIESEMEYER   BILL BIESEMEYER

ARIZONA BOAT WORKS
FOR
Everything in Boat and Motor Work
Fibre Glassing • Painting and Refinishing
Custom Built Boats • Inboard Installation
We Service All Makes of Outboard Motors

PHONE AL 4-3731   1009 WEST TAYLOR
                         PHOENIX, ARIZONA

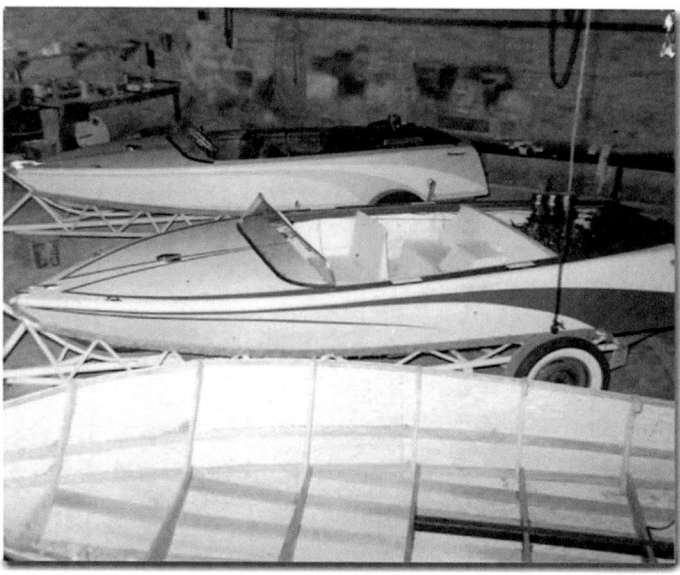

Blast From The Past

The Way It Was

This was actually a 1956 boat with no hydraulic clutch. It is amazing that this wooden boat is still going after almost 50 years. They were built good!

Hot Boat takes a stroll down performance-boat memory lane.
by Bob Brown

Performance has always been an integral part of the boating scene. Ever since the likes of Gar Wood and Chris Smith nearly a century ago, the pursuit of speed on the water has been a compulsion and a challenge irresistible to many.

Like many industries, however, performance boating officially entered its modern era shortly after the conclusion of World War II. The U.S. postwar economy boomed quickly as the civilian population was anxious to resume a more normal, nonrestrictive lifestyle and to once again enjoy leisure-time pleasures, one of which was to go boating.

Prior to the 1950s, boats were a product made almost exclusively of wood. Fiberglass was still a rather exotic material which didn't find its way into the mainstream of boat-building until a few years later. That meant boats were still handcrafted, one at a time, by incredibly skilled finish carpenters. Chris Craft, which was founded in 1874, remained the dominate force in the marketplace in the immediate post-war era, even when it came to owning a real "speedboat" thanks to its continuing production of various models of its popular "racing Chris" line. These sleek and lower-profile mahogany beauties were soon mated with the emerging automotive V-8 engines of the late-1940s from the likes of Cadillac, Lincoln and Chrysler. The combination of Detroit powerplants and Chris Craft expertise set the tone and standard for the performance-boating revolution about to occur.

In the years immediately following the war, outboard motor production from Mercury, Evinrude and Johnson resumed in a hurry. The affordability of these new and larger horsepower two-strokes soon found their way into the hands of performance enthusiasts. Flashy all-wood outboard runabouts in the 12- to 15-foot range rapidly became a status symbol for the middle class in the early-1950s. Even famous Hollywood cowboy Roy Rogers was captivated by the new sport, becoming an avid outboard racer with his twin Merc-powered Yellow Jacket hull.

At about that same time, a few ingenious hot-rodders and dry-lakebed racers from the Southwest allowed their innovative juices to overflow into the performance-boating business. Not content to let the classic Chris Crafts rule the local lakes and the Colorado River, pioneers like Joe Mandella, Rich Hallett, Fred Wickens and Rusty Biesemeyer soon started designing and building a new and different style of flatbottom inboard runabout that later became known as the "SK." Still made from wood, these lower silhouette recreational ski boats had a noticeably longer deck, wider beam. Power for these new-breed "SKs" was now supplied to the propeller using a V-drive gearbox which drove off the front of the engine with an output shaft that ran back toward the transom and out through the bottom of the hull instead of a conventional in-line direct drive. The V-drive concept put the engine farther aft in the boat for better high-speed weight distribution, better turning, and a shallower propshaft angle. The aft engine placement also opened up extra room inside the main cockpit for more passengers.

Until the mid-1950s, the manufacturing of performance boats pretty much remained a very labor-intensive one-at-a-time operation thanks to the craftsmanship needed to cut, shape, sand, screw and glue hundreds of pieces of wood together in order to build a boat. Nick Barron of Hallett Boats remembers the revolution that was soon to come. "Back then, we called

A 1954 15' Biesemeyer wooden ski racer with a Studebaker engine and a hydraulic clutch.

Arizona Boat Works 1957-1958
The History of the 16-foot Biesemeyer Boat

I quit the boat business in early 1957 and went back to work in a cabinet shop because we ran out of orders for the wooden boat. Rusty got some more money from Milton, then started the mock-up for the first 16-foot fiberglass ski boat.

A mock-up is where you build the form of the boat. It can be built out of any material. We sprayed resin on the mock-up and laid many layers of fiberglass over the mock-up to create the mold. After that was done, a lot of fine sanding, polishing and waxing had to be done on the mold. We then sprayed a colored resin, called gel coat, into the mold. So, the boat was actually painted before it was built. Then we laid many layers of fiberglass, cloth, mat and resin into the mold to make the boat. When we started making the first 16-footers, we didn't know how much material to use, so we used way too much and that is why they were so strong. Today people are finding these old boats and restoring them because of their strength.

After a couple of months, Rusty made me go back to work with him at the boat shop to help him finish the mock-up of the fiberglass ski boat. We hired two fiberglass workers named Mike and Armando. Rusty and I made the molds and then made the first all fiberglass 16-foot inboard Biesemeyer Boat. This was the first all fiberglass boat that was strong enough for a big engine. Ski racing was very popular at that time and these boats were absolutely perfect for fast ski boats. For a while, Rusty and I could not build enough of them.

At the end of each ski race, there would be a fast boat race without the skier. Rusty was always determined to have one of his boats win the fast boat race at the end of the day. This eventually evolved into the flat-bottom class of racing boats in the APBA (American Power Boat Association).

In 1958, Rusty and I made the first all fiberglass 16-foot outboard boat. It really performed well. We made a few, then Rusty's boat business went broke so he borrowed some more money and we moved the company to East McDowell Road in Phoenix and changed the name to Biesemeyer Plastics, Inc. This is where we built the Pied Piper that won many ski races and a lot of fast hot boat races. It was also where we built the first 14-foot outboard Biesemeyer.

Rusty at our first boat show in 1958 soon after we started building the 16-foot Biesemeyer Boats. It was at Phoenix Marine on East McDowell in Phoenix.

This was at a race in Parker, Arizona. The boat is a 16-foot Biesemeyer built for Jay Barker. Mike Biesemeyer, Rusty's son, is walking on the dock. Jay Barker is on the dock and his wife, Phyllis, is in the center of the boat.

Rusty and Bill beside one of their new 16-foot outboards.

The first 16-foot outboard out of the mold.

This boat was built for Jacque Pettijohn. It was called the Pied Piper. It won more ski races and hot boat races than any other 16-foot Biesemeyer Boat.

One of the 16-foot Biesemeyer Boats.

16-foot Biesemeyer Boats at the Parker race

About 1958

Bill Biesemeyer

Race car driver Jim Bryan with cigar

Biesemeyer 16-footers at the Parker race

Cost Guard using Biesemeyer Boats

Dusenberry rustles up the Colorado's waters as he puts his boat into tight turn.

Miller cruises the river in his high-speed fiber glass boat.

This 16-foot Biesemeyer Boat was used by the Coast Guard in about 1958 or 1959.

Decal used on Biesemeyer Boats in 1957.

In late 1957 this chrome plate was being used on Biesemeyer Boats.

Restored Boats

These are 16-foot Biesemeyer Boats that were restored or are in the process of being restored many years later.

We did not take nearly enough pictures of our boats.

We were looking for more pictures. On the internet in 2008, we ran across a man in Gilbert, Arizona who owned the unrestored 1958 16-foot Biesemeyer outboard on these two pages. We were delighted to find this boat because it was in such fine condition for a 50-year-old boat. I called the man and we had a nice conversation. He said it was fine to use his pictures.

This boat has the original color and it has custom upholstery. It is a beautiful Biesemeyer Boat.

Biesemeyer Boat & Plastic Co., Inc. 1959-1960

There were only three models of the Biesemeyer Boat built between 1959 and 1960.

First was the 14-foot outboard that was a beautiful little boat and performed flawlessly. We also made four 14-foot inboards, but they never performed really well so we stopped making them.

The second boat was Rusty's 18-foot double-bubble inboard deck boat. We called it the double-bubble because it had two raised sections on the deck. It was a beautiful boat but it did not perform really well.

The third boat was a 4-point hydroplane inboard that I built after Rusty left. It had two sponsons on the front and two on the back so it had a tunnel that went all the way through.

Rusty mismanaged the company and ran it into debt. The people he owed money to took over Biesemeyer Plastics. Rusty left because he lost control of the company, but I stayed there to run it.

Jacques Pettijohn bought one of the 4-point hydroplanes, then Tony Bedims modified the hull and set up the engine. In 1962 it broke the quarter-mile speed record at 125.62 mph.

In 1961, I left the company and went back to work in a cabinet shop. Biesemeyer Plastics operated for over a year without Rusty or me, then it closed down.

Name plate used on Biesemeyer Boats starting in 1959

Biesemeyer 18'

L.O.A. 18 Feet, BEAM 90 Inches, FIBERGLASS — MOLDED COLORS. SEE IT NOW Booth #H-H 6-7-8 and #121 Los Angeles Boat Show and your local Biesemeyer dealer.

ANOTHER OUTSTANDING SKI BOAT BY BIESEMEYER

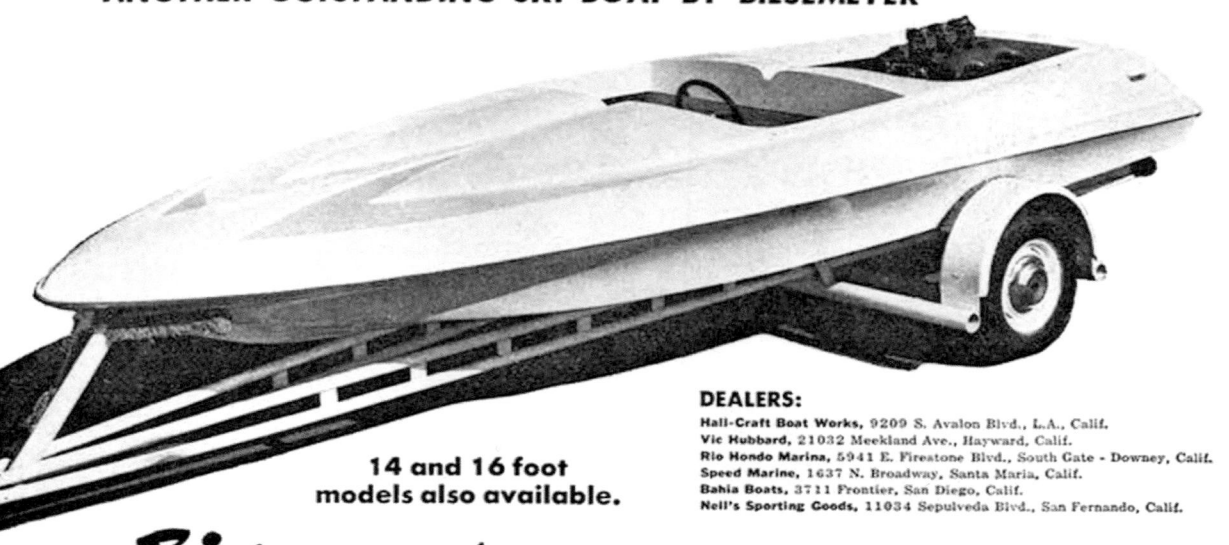

14 and 16 foot models also available.

DEALERS:
Hall-Craft Boat Works, 9209 S. Avalon Blvd., L.A., Calif.
Vic Hubbard, 21032 Meekland Ave., Hayward, Calif.
Rio Hondo Marina, 5941 E. Firestone Blvd., South Gate - Downey, Calif.
Speed Marine, 1637 N. Broadway, Santa Maria, Calif.
Bahia Boats, 3711 Frontier, San Diego, Calif.
Neil's Sporting Goods, 11034 Sepulveda Blvd., San Fernando, Calif.

Biesemeyer BOAT & PLASTIC CO., INC.
PHOENIX, ARIZONA

A customer wanted a 14-foot inboard boat, so Rusty and I made an inboard deck for the outboard bottom. Only about four were made because it was not a very good boat.

This 14-foot Biesemeyer Boat belongs to John Stiller of Colorado. It was probably built in 1959 and was in terrible condition when he bought it in 2009. He loved the classic lines and decided to do a full restoration, which took two years. When bought, the boat included crash padding inside the cockpit areas and a stainless steel skeg (fin) on the bottom so it was probably used in circle racing. His family now uses it extensively during the summer months for skiing and recreation. John also participates in classic boating events with the Rocky Mountain Classics Boat Club.

Before restoration

After restoration

West Coast BOATING NEWS

"The Boater's Newspaper"

Friday, October 30, 1959 — Volume 2, Number 7

MODEL Carol Lee wheels the new all-fiberglass Biesemeyer outboard runabout over calm waters in front of Frank's Small Boat Launching in Long Beach Harbor. Carol, incidentally, is not only a very pretty young lady. She also is an excellent boat driver and had several nice things to say about the handling qualities of the Biesemeyer.

Staff photo

WEST COAST BOATING
10960½ W. Pico Blvd.
Los Angeles 64, California

Biesemeyer BOATS

A truly new concept in boating

"You Couldn't Find a Better Boat for the Motor of Your Choice"

14 ft. Outboard. . $895.

16 ft. Outboard. . $1195.

DEALERS:

Bahia Boat Works	3711 Frontier St., San Diego, Calif.
Boat Barn	3165 E. Pacific Coast Hwy., Long Beach, Calif.
Bohners Boats & Motors	4729 N. Blackstone, Fresno, Calif.
Escondido Sport Center	237 E. Grand Ave., Escondido, Calif.
W. K. Klessig Co.	8766 Valley Blvd., Rosemead, Calif.
Norm's Western Marine	5060 Venice Blvd., Los Angeles, Calif.
Niel's Sporting Goods	13352 Van Nuys Blvd., Pacoima, Calif.
Sportsmans Trading Post	1042 E. Highland Ave., San Bernardino, Calif.
Sunset Marine Center	California Ave., Bakersfield, Calif.
Valley Boats & Motors	Hwy 60/70, Blythe, Calif.
Willis Hunt	320 W. Coast Hwy., Newport Beach, Calif.
Valley Marine	1326 Harding Way, Stockton, Calif.
Victory Sporting Goods	Coachella, Calif.

BAHIA BOAT WORKS
3711 Frontier St.
San Diego — AC 2-0363

DEALER INQUIRIES INVITED

Hall Craft Boat Works in Los Angeles, California was the best Biesemeyer Boat dealer. The others listed in this add were good dealers in California.

Bahia Boat Works was a dealer in San Diego, California. It was one of the better dealers and sold a lot of Biesemeyer outboards. My family and I were invited to San Diego to demonstrate the 16-foot outboard for an article in a magazine. Rusty didn't go because he wasn't working at Biesemeyer Boats at the time.

Biesemeyer Boats in a Los Angeles boat show in 1959
16-foot inboard
14-foot inboard
18-foot double-bubble inboard

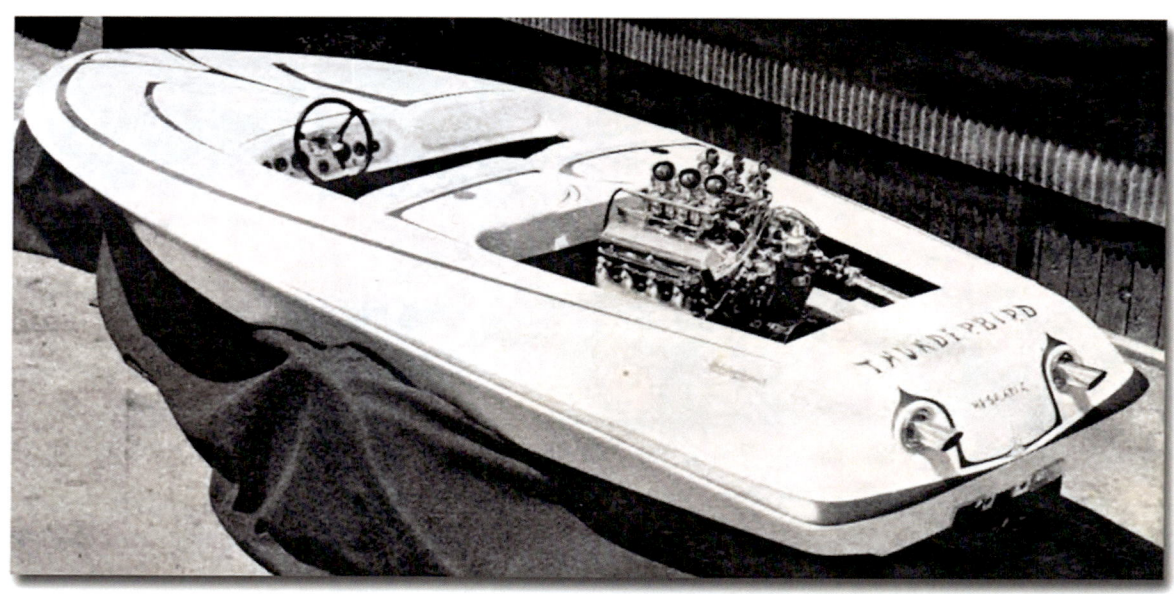

18-foot double-bubble inboard

This 18-foot double-bubble inboard is shown on the showroom floor at Phoenix Marine in 1960. Frank Weaver did the upholstery work on this beautiful boat. He did most of the upholstery work on Biesemeyer Boats from 1957-1961.

Rusty's Carribean 1960-1962

Rusty left Phoenix and went to Texas in 1960. He worked for a friend building and selling swimming pool equipment. While he was there, he built the mock-up for the Carribean, an 17-foot inboard ski boat. Rusty gave his boat that name because he loved the word Carribean. This was Rusty's most beautiful boat, but unfortunately, it didn't perform really well.

In early 1962, Rusty came back to Tempe, Arizona where he found someone who would loan him some money. He used the money to start a boat business to make the Carribean. He made a few, then ran out of money so he went to work for someone else and was no longer building boats.

Jacques Pettijohn had previously bought one of the Biesemeyer 4-point hydroplanes, then Tony Tedims modified the hull and set up the engine. In 1962 it broke the quarter-mile speed record at 125.62 mph at an APBA race at Marine Stadium in Long Beach, California.

While Rusty was working on the Carribean, I worked for Dave Jackson in his cabinet shop. I moved to Show Low, Arizona in 1962 where I started a cabinet shop called Biesemeyer Cabinet & Millwork and operated it for three years.

Rusty and I did not build boats together again until 1965.

Making the Carribean

Shipping some Carribeans

Rusty's Carribean

Jacque Pettijohn at the helm of Wrangler, a 4-point Biesemeyer hydroplane, designed by Bill Biesemeyer. It held the world quarter-mile drag record in 1962 at 125.62 at Long Beach Stadium.

The new APBA record holder in the quarter-mile go is Jack Pettijohn's Biesemeyer hull "Wrangler." Sporting an injected blown Chrysler on fuel "Wrangler" turned 125.62 at Long Beach Stadium.

Unfortunately, I did not have any pictures of the 4-point hydroplane. But we found these pictures of the same boat on the Internet. They were posted by someone who didn't know what kind of boat it was and wanted to restore it.

Biesemeyer Marine 1965-1966

My cabinet shop in Show Low went broke. Rusty had a shop on East Van Buren in Phoenix called Biesemeyer Marine where he was building a new deep-V 17-foot inboard and outboard boat. I started driving down from Show Low during the week to work for Rusty and going home on the weekends so my children could finish high school in Snowflake.

The inboard version of the 17-foot Biesemeyer Boat

They were jet-powered inboards

Left is the outboard version of the 17-footer

Below is a custom 17-foot Biesemeyer outboard with a high transom that we built specifically to run the Parker marathon race

Biesemeyer Boats, Inc. 1966-1970

In 1966, Rusty started another shop on 16th Street and Oak in Phoenix. The name of the business was Biesemeyer Boats, Inc. I worked for him at that shop and installed some engines in the previous 17-foot boats. He was building the mock-up for the 20-foot day cruiser. The first 20-foot day cruiser was a flatbottom version.

In 1968, Rusty rented another place on West Buckeye Road in Phoenix. There we made the molds for the day cruiser. We only built about three of the flatbottom day cruisers, then started working on the mock-up for the deep-V version of the day cruiser. It was obvious a deep-V was needed because the boats needed jet propulsion and the deep-V worked better.

While we were working at West Buckeye Road, Rusty, Julian Pettengill, and Ron Eadie were working on the bottom molds for the K-boats at the shop on 16th Street and Oak. Then they moved the K-boat bottom molds to a shop on 711 Jefferson in Phoenix.

Rusty, Julian, and Ron altered the bottom of an aqua craft boat to make the bottom molds for the K-boat. It was highly modified. They added six inches to the transom, changed the chimes to drop chimes, and put strakes on the bottom. It was very unusual for a flat-bottom boat to have strakes, but they knew it would stop the boat from sticking to the water.

Julian Pettengill was a business man who was very interested in our boats and would hang around the shop a lot. Because Julian wanted a K-boat for racing, he supplied money so that he and Rusty could build the K-boat molds.

After we started production on the 20-foot day cruiser, Rusty and Julian worked nights making the mock-up and molds for the K-boat deck. Every morning when I came to work, I had the crew help me clean up the mess that was made the night before.

The first Biesemeyer K-boats were made in 1967. The second K-boat we made was Julian Pettengill's Coldfire. Rusty and Julian designed the bottom of Coldfire and Rusty designed the top. Later, Julian altered the deck to make it shorter so his legs wouldn't get caught under the dashboard if the boat crashed.

This is the first 20-foot deep-V coming out of the mold

20-foot Deep-V Day Cruiser

This is the best ski boat that we ever made. We sold a lot of them and they were excellent for taking the whole family skiing because they were carpeted under the deck so you could go underneath the deck and lie down.

All of these boats were jet powered, which was very good for pulling skiers out of the water. The Berkeley jet units were made by the same people who made pumps for water wells. They sucked the water in from the bottom of the boat and with great pressure pushed it out the back of the jet unit.

20-foot Day Cruiser deck

Rusty Biesemeyer is driving this boat, with Jerry Huntley and Dan Biesemeyer riding behind him.

Biesemeyer Boats

1970 BIESEMEYER HIGH PERFORMANCE DEEP-V SKI AND FAMILY CRUISER

SPECIFICATIONS

Centerline length 20' 2" / Beam 93" / Transom width 84" / Transom height 30" / Maximum hull depth 40" / Color-matched carpeting / Beautiful wood-grained side storage panels cover roomy ski and storage areas / General vinyl all-weather folding or full-length seating / Choice of ten solid colors or twenty available metalflake combinations at slight additional cost.

PROPULSION POWER & INSTRUMENTS

Oldsmobile marine engine, 455 cubic inch displacement / Optional 365 or 390 horsepower / 12 volt solid state alternator with built-in regulator / Heavy duty battery / Bilge pump / Bilge exhaust blower / Keyed ignition switch / Tachometer, alternator output, oil pressure and water temperature guages /
Berkely Jet-Drive Model J-12JB-H standard unit, stainless steel impeller available at extra cost / Morse single level throttle and shift control / Steermaster Mk II steering control with optional color steering wheel /

CONSTRUCTION

Polyester reenforced fiberglass outer hull with major laminations up to one inch thick. Four vertical grain select Douglas Fir stringers cut from choice 2" by 6" lumber. Engine and passenger deck of ½" marine plywood completely glassed top and bottom with two-ounce material and seven ounce cloth.

STANDARD AND OPTIONAL ITEMS

Standard equipment includes two built-in 17 gallon tanks with sight gauges, passenger assist grip, engine cover safety support, two 22" wide folding front seats or full-width back-to-back seats in black or white, ski-tow bracket.

Optional equipment available at slight extra cost includes 390 HP engine, stainless steel impellor on Jet-pump, 35" wide folding passenger seat, metalflake color combinations, deck hardware, bow & stern lights, cigarette lighter, spot light, windshield, top, stereo & speakers, fire extinguisher, glovebox and a large variety of marine accessories.

Manufactured by

Biesemeyer Boats

A Division of
WESTERN PRODUCTS, INC.
2827 WEST BUCKEYE ROAD
PHOENIX, ARIZONA 85009
Phone (602) 278-8044
278-4312

Sold by

The name of the business changed from Western Products, Inc. to Biesemeyer Boats, Inc. in July 1970.

The first K-boat

powerboat PERFORMANCE REPORT
Biesemeyer DAY CRUISER

The art of building day cruisers has come a long way in the past several years. It wasn't too long ago that the only name that came to mind when speaking of one of these lightweight cruisers was Campbell.

It is pleasant to run across a design that isn't a copy and incorporates some fresh and new ideas into its construction. Biesemeyer has always had an excellent reputation as a quality boat manufacturer, and the new 20' day cruiser follows in the tradition of his other hulls. The word that best describes the boat is sanitary; sanitary in design, in installation and interior layout. Our test boat was a beautiful orange and gold metal flake. This particular model is available in a choice of six solid colors or an optional 20 metal flake colors.

The center line length is 20' 2", beam 93", hull depth 35", transom width 86", transom height 21". Seating was via four back-to-back buckets, upholstered in a white all-weather vinyl upholstery, wood-grained side storage panels flanked both sides of the interior, and the boat is completely carpeted in an indoor-outdoor color matched carpeting.

Hull construction is in the Biesemeyer tradition with polyester reinforced hand laid-up fiberglass hull, with the major lamination up to 1" thick. There are four two-inch vertical grain Douglas fir stringers sandwiched between the major bottom laminations, plus ½" marine plywood forming the engine passenger deck which is completely glassed, underside and topside using 2-oz. material with 7½-oz. cloth.

Our test boat was equipped with a 455 Olds using Nicson Marine conversion. Standard equipment includes 12-volt solid-state alternator with built-in voltage regulator, heavy-duty battery, 12-volt bilge ventilation blower and key ignition switch. The engine is housed in a two-piece contoured fiberglass engine compartment.

We were running a Berkeley jet unit with a single lever shift and throttle control. The same model is also available in a V-drive installation using a Crusader V-drive. Steering is via a Steermaster Mark II control and cable unit. Instrumentation included tachometer, oil pressure gauge, water temperature gauge and alternator gauge. In order to get a speed reading we hooked up a Keller water speed indicator, placing the pickup on the bell unit of the Berkeley Jet Drive. The fuel is housed in twin 14-gallon built-in glass tanks; Biesemeyer very cleverly left two slots in the side panels to provide sight gauges for each tank. The boat was carried on an A/M standard tadem trailer.

The hull itself has 17½ degrees of dead rise at the transom and carried three longitudinal strakes. The bare hull includes seats, and steering weighs 1,150 lbs. The jet unit checks in at 100 lbs. with a 455 Olds with marine conversion, 750 lbs. Our test weight, including fuel, was 2,250 lbs.

We decided to give the Biesemeyer an ocean test since our freshwater test sight turned out to be a little too calm, and we wanted to give the 20-footer a good run in some choppy water. The boat was extremely easy to launch which is a pleasure these days. Too many boats are being built without much thought given to how they are going to be taken off the trailer. Moving out past the breakwater we ran into our first noticeable problem — low-speed handling. Jet boats do not handle well at idle speeds. Since our test boat was not equipped with an auxiliary rudder which would have helped, the boat required constant steer-

(Continued on Page 30)

BIESEMEYER *(Continued from Page 29)*

ing correction all the way up through 2,000 rpms. Even at 2,000 it is not steady enough for hands-off driving. The jet units do not put our enough thrust at low rpm to keep the boat steady.

The passenger was supplied with a grab rail which comes in very handy when the going gets rough. We did notice, however, that the grab rail could have been positioned a little further to the passenger's right for complete comfort. Another point, if the boat is going to be used in the ocean on a regular basis, it might be wise to install foot braces which do much to add to driving comfort. The steering wheel for a 6'2" driver is a little high, something that could easily be remedied.

Seating comfort in the 20-footer was excellent. There was no elbow contact on the gunnal when both hands were on the wheel; this is one of the few boats that I have found this to be the case.

The installation on the 20-footer was beautiful; the entire boat had a clean and uncluttered appearance. Biesemeyer gave great attention to detail with polished aluminum molding around all edges.

The boat was virtually unaffected by shifting of weight which comes in very handy when you have kids running from one side to the other when dead in the water. Once we had her out into the open water, we were immediately impressed, as we always are, with the acceleration that the Berkeley Jet unit provides. Our test boat was extremely light, hence in our tight turns the boat did have a tendency to lean, although it never had a feeling of sliding or skipping. It would merely find its groove and lean into the turn.

While the Biesemeyer did have a tendency to lean in the turns, it never gave an indication of skipping or sliding. It would find its groove and hold it throughout the turn.

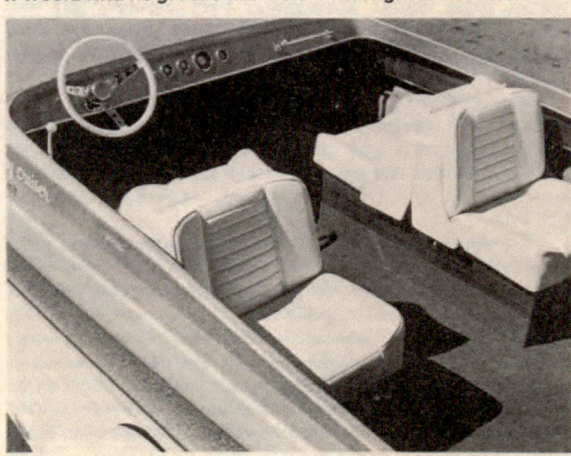

The interior layout and design of the Biesemeyer was especially roomy and very sanitary.

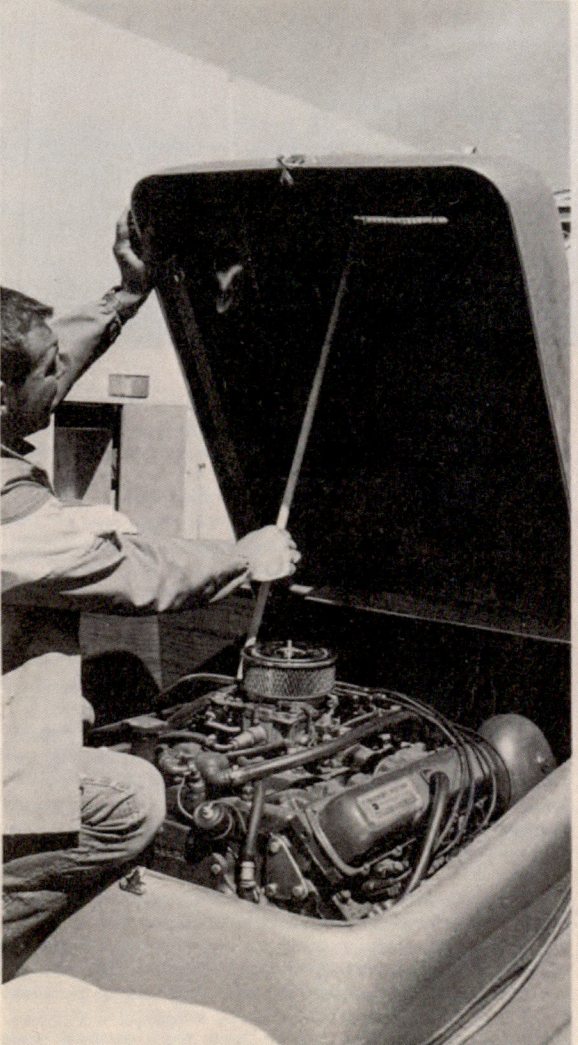

The 455 Olds was housed in a contoured fiberglass engine compartment. Our test boat was a prototype so the engine hatch was held open by a stick. All production models have spring-loaded hatch covers.

One thing we were impressed with in the Biesemeyer is the fact that it did not glue itself in at higher speeds. It might be wise at this point to review some bottom characteristics to understand the capabilities of the Biesemeyer bottom. With the exception of good SK shapes, prop-driven hulls carry a hook or concave shape longitudinally from the transom ending several feet forward. This hook keeps the bow down and avoids porpoising. Manufacturers put this hook in their hull in order to keep people out of trouble especially when the manufacturer is not sure what is going to power his boat. Let me add, however, that a hook does not usually make for high performance. For speed, it is generally desirable to have a bottom that will either porpoise slightly due to a rocker or is on the verge of porpoising. It usually is not difficult to stop porpoising, but if a boat is glued into too much, it will never go. Generally SK bottoms have between ¼" to ⅜" rocker in four feet of bottom, and the porpoising is controlled with adjustable cavitation plates.

Jets, however, impose a different problem. Most jet boats have a natural glued-in characteristic. This is caused by the suction of the pump inlet, plus, in the case of the Berkeley unit, downward thrust of the jet nozzle. This will

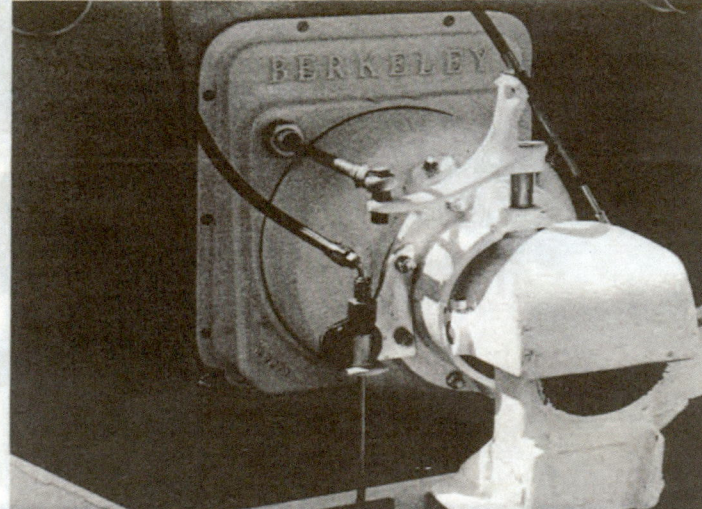

We installed a Keller water-speed indicator to the bell housing of the Berkeley jet unit.

The Berkeley jet unit coupled to the 455 Olds gave the 20-footer exceptional acceleration.

BIESEMEYER

tend to raise the transom and drop the bow.

The Biesemeyer bottom shape handles the jet unit ideally. It allowed the boat to ride free and yet did not porpoise, an amiable combination to say the least.

Top speed on our test boat in a moderate chop with small white caps was 44-mph. There is no doubt the boat would run 5 to 6-mph faster in calmer water as we were continually plagued with our intake pulling free of the water. Our test boat actually was a little lightweight for ideal ocean running conditions but would be ideal in inland waters. If you were interested in making trips into the open sea with this hull, it could be easily beefed up and given the additional weight necessary. The 17½ degrees of dead rise gives the boat a fairly soft ride in choppy seas. While this really isn't enough V for heavy seas, it's the perfect answer for family boating. At least you're not constantly plagued with a hull that either falls off when running free or hunts once the nose is dropped in the water.

The new Biesemeyer 20-footer should be a fine inland water day cruiser and with a few modifications could probably be made into a better-than-average offshore express cruise.

Arizona Ski Boats 1971-1972

The second K-boat we built was for Julian Pettengill and was named Coldfire. It was made with balsa wood squares laminated on the bottom of the boat to keep the bottom stiff and the weight down. Andy Cassell made V-drive gear boxes for boats and he showed Julian how to use a straight drive line with no U-joints. Julian's Coldfire was one of the first boats that had spring-loaded cavitation plates. It was fuel injected and didn't have a supercharger.

Julian started racing Coldfire in the flatbottom class and won practically every race, which made the sales of the Biesemeyer K-boat very good. In 1971 he raced in Seattle, Washington and won the national championship.

Unfortunately, Rusty was a very poor business man. In 1971 we found out that he had the molds mortgaged to man named Ken Overton. Apparently Rusty was very behind on paying when he was supposed to. One day Ken Overton came over with a crew of people and they proceeded to take the molds out of the shop and put them in a lot next door so a truck could pick them up. When Ken started to pick up the molds for the K-boat, Julian Pettengill said that he paid for the K-boat molds, he owned them and Ken could not take them. I was surprised that Ken and his crew didn't think to take the patterns for cutting the wooden parts of the boats. They also didn't take the gas tank molds, engine cover molds and other things.

Rusty was broke and no longer in business. After the molds were picked up, Julian and his business partner, Paul Edwards, were sitting with me in the building asking what they were going to do. Since Julian owned the K-boat molds, I suggested that they start a new business making Biesemeyer Boats in that same building. They talked about it for a while and said they would have to come up with enough money, but they would do it if I would promise to work for them. I said I would.

Up the street on Buckeye Road was a dairy farmer who had bought one of the 20-foot day cruisers. Julian went to him and asked if he would let us use his boat to make a new mold and in return we would give him a brand-new boat. He said sure. Then we got a 17-foot Biesemeyer Boat and made a mold out of it. We were now in business building boats and we called the company Arizona Ski Boats.

We continued making four boats: the 20-foot day cruiser, the 18-foot jet boat, the 17-foot outboard, and the 17.5-foot K-boat.

In 1972, after a Bubby Wilton supercharged motor was put in Coldfire, Julian set the kilo record with a speed 127.850 mph and won the Regatta of Champions.

This is Julian's Coldfire in 1971 when he won the national championship.

Julian set the kilo record in Coldfire in 1972 with a supercharged motor.

OFF. (602) 278-8044   RES. (602) 272-1688

Arizona Ski Boats
BUILDER OF
Biesemeyer Boats

BILL BIESEMEYER

2827 W. BUCKEYE RD.
PHOENIX, ARIZ. 85009

Biesemeyer Boats

1971 BIESEMEYER HIGH PERFORMANCE DEEP V OUTBOARD AND INBOARD RUNABOUT

Specifications

Length 16 feet / Beam 78 inches / Transom width 62 inches / Transom height 21 inches / Color matched carpeting / Back to back vinyl all weather seats /

Outboard Models

Standard equipment - Steermaster MKII steering controls / Seats / Carpet /

Inboard Models

Standard equipment - Berkley jet drive / Steermaster MKII / Seats / Carpet / Tachometer, alternator output, oil pressure and water temperature gauges / Fiberglass built in gas tanks 24 gallon /

Manufactured by

Biesemeyer Boats
2827 WEST BUCKEYE ROAD
PHOENIX, ARIZONA 85009
Phone (602) 278-8044
278-4312

Sold by

Biesemeyer Boats

1971 BIESEMEYER HIGH PERFORMANCE DEEP-V SKI AND FAMILY CRUISER

SPECIFICATIONS

Length 21 feet / Beam 93" / Transom width 84" / Transom height 30" / Maximum hull depth 40" / Color-matched carpeting / Beautiful wood-grained side storage panels cover roomy ski and storage areas / General vinyl all-weather folding or full-length seating / Choice of twenty solid colors (or twenty available metalflake combinations at slight additional cost).

PROPULSION POWER & INSTRUMENTS

Lincoln marine engine, 460 cubic inch or Oldsmobile marine engine, 455 cubic inch displacement / 12 volt solid state alternator with built-in regulator / Heavy duty battery / Bilge pump / Bilge exhaust blower / Keyed ignition switch / Tachometer, alternator output, oil pressure and water temperature gauges /
Berkely Jet-Drive Model J-12JB-H standard unit, stainless steel impeller available at extra cost / Morse single level throttle and shift control / Steermaster Mk II steering control with optional color steering wheel /

CONSTRUCTION

Polyester reenforced fiberglass outer hull with major laminations up to one inch thick. Four vertical grain select Douglas Fir stringers cut from choice 2" by 6" lumber. Engine and passenger deck of ½" marine plywood completely glassed top and bottom with two-ounce material and seven ounce cloth.

STANDARD AND OPTIONAL ITEMS

Standard equipment includes two built-in 17 gallon tanks with sight gauges, passenger assist grip, engine cover safety support, two 22" wide folding front seats or full-width back-to-back seats in black or white, ski-tow bracket.

Optional equipment available at slight extra cost includes 390 HP Oldsmobile engine, stainless steel impeller or Jet-pump, 35" wide folding passenger seat, metalflake color combinations, deck hardware, bow & stern lights, cigarette lighter, spot light, windshield, top, stereo & speakers, fire extinguisher, glovebox and a large variety of marine accessories.

Manufactured by

Biesemeyer Boats

2827 WEST BUCKEYE ROAD
PHOENIX, ARIZONA 85009
Phone (602) 278-8044
278-4312

Sold by

craftsmanship
quality
reliability
style
performance

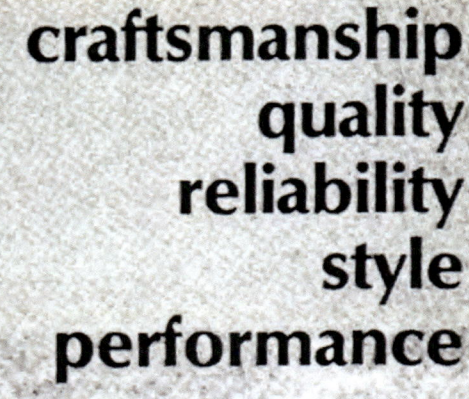

...with all these features,
it can only be a

Biesemeyer Boat
ALL NEW FOR 1971

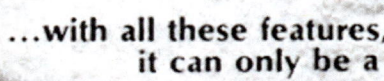

16' deep V-bottom outboard

18' semi V-bottom inboard

... but most important, is Pride. The Pride we take in creating the 1971 Biesemeyer Family Cruiser is second to none. She is constructed of lightweight, long-lasting, low maintenance fiberglass, designed with a super sleek, deep V-bottom, jet powered and great for water skiing or cruising. Biesemeyer Boats, one step ahead of the future, take pride in introducing our 16' deep V-bottom outboard and the all-new, exciting 18' semi V-bottom inboard ski/race boat... both designed to become the tops in their class.

This is what you have been asking for... your thoughts and ideas guided us in creating these 2 new designs. We're excited about our line of boats... we want you to be excited with us. Write for complete information and we'll send you a free key chain float... as the first step in putting you in a 1971 Biesemeyer Boat.

 FREE

2827 W. Buckeye Rd. / Phoenix, Arizona 85009 / (602) 278-4312

Choice dealerships still available.

Biesemeyer Boats

1972 IMPROVED HIGH PERFORMANCE DEEP-V SKI AND FAMILY CRUISER

LIST PRICE $5,695.00*

SPECIFICATIONS:

Length 21 feet / Beam 93" / Transom width 84" / Transom height 30" / Maximum hull depth 40" / Carpeting Beautiful wood-grained side storage panels cover roomy ski and storage areas / General vinyl all-weather folding or full-width seating / Choice of solid colors (or twenty available metalflake combinations at slight additional cost).

PROPULSION POWER & INSTRUMENTS:

Standard equipment (based on availability) plus Ford-Lincoln marine engine, 460 cubic inch or Oldsmobile marine engine, 455 cubic inch / 12 volt solid state alternator with built-in regulator / Heavy duty battery Bilge pump / Bilge exhaust blower / Keyed ignition switch / Tachometer, alternator output, oil pressure and water temperature gauges / Berkely Jet-Drive Model J-12JB-H standard unit / Morse single level throttle and shift control / Steermaster Mk II steering control with optional color steering wheel / Optional engines include 400 and 454 Chevrolet, 427 Ford Cobra, 390 HP Olds 455.

CONSTRUCTION:

Polyester reenforced fiberglass outer hull with major laminations up to one inch thick. Four vertical grain select Douglas Fir stringers cut from choice 2" by 6" lumber. Engine and passenger deck of 1/2" marine plywood completely glassed top and bottom with two-ounce material and seven ounce cloth.

STANDARD AND OPTIONAL ITEMS:

Standard equipment includes two built-in 17 gallon tanks with sight gauges, passenger assist grip, engine cover safety support, two 20" wide folding front seats or full-width back-to-back seats in black or white, ski-tow bracket.

Optional equipment available at slight extra cost includes stainless steel impeller or Jet-pump, 35" wide folding passenger seat, metalflake color combinations, deck hardware, bow and stern lights, cigarette lighter, spot light, windshield, top, stereo and speakers, fire extinguisher, glovebox and a large variety of marine accessories.

F.O.B. Phoenix, Arizona
*Price subject to Increase after, January 1972.

ARIZONA SKI BOATS

builder of

Biesemeyer Boats

2827 West Buckeye Road ■ Phoenix, Arizona 85009
Phone: (602) 278-8044

Arizona Ski Boats 1973

Biesemeyer Boats had a really good year in 1973. We were building and selling several different models of Biesemeyer Boats and we had a great crew working for the business.

In May 1973, our shop moved to 414 South 59th Avenue in Phoenix. Julian Pettengill's

partner, Paul Edwards, and I were running the day-to-day operations of the shop at Arizona Ski Boats. I got to know Paul really well, but didn't know Julian well at that time because I wasn't working with him everyday. The next page is from a brochure of some of the boats we were making at that time.

Julian and Coldfire won the Nationals and went on to set a five-mile competition record of 102.857 mph. No other boat, not even the hydroplanes, had ever gone that fast on that size course. Julian and Coldfire held that record until the 1990s. He also was the high-point U.S. champion and won the Regatta of Champions in 1973.

The September 1992 issue of *Powerboat Magazine* wrote about Julian in an article titled "Breaking the Barriers," which said: "[In 1973,] Julian Pettengill's K-class Coldfire circles a 5-mile course at 102.867, the fastest speed yet by any inboard flatbottom or hydroplane in competition." This record held until 1992 when it was broken by Gordon Jennings' son in another Biesemeyer Boat named Freedom. He set the record at 104.950 mph. Also in 1992, Jennings' son held the kilo record in the same boat at 146.649.

Coldfire had a fuel injected engine and ran 25% nitro-methane.

"The Tahoe"
21 FOOT DAY CRUISER

"The Ultimate in Family Ski Boats"

This luxury ski boat comes standard equipped with Oldsmobile's 455 cubic inch marine engine/ indoor-outdoor carpet/ vinyl all weather folding or full width seating/ woodgrained side storage panels/ soundproof insulated engine cover/ two built-in 17 gallon fuel compartment with sight guages/ bilge pump/ fully customed instrument dash/ ski tow brackets/ Mark II Streemaster controls/ and Berkeley or Jacuzzi jet drive proplulsion.

Specifications: Length - 21 feet/ beam - 93 inches/ transom width - 84 inches/ transom height - 30 inches/ maximum hull depth - 40 inches/ approximate weight - 2500 pounds.

"The Apache"
18 FOOT DEEP-V RUNABOUT

"For High Performance At Its Best"

This family fun boat comes standard equipped with Oldsmobile's 455 cubic inch marine engine/ two back - to - back vinyl seats/ two built - in 16 gallon fuel tanks with sight guages/ ski tow brackets/ insulated engine shroud/ fully customed instrumented dash/ Mark II Steermaster control/ and Berkeley or Jacuzzi jet drive propulsion.

Specifications: Length - 18 feet 6 inches/ beam - 86 inches/ transom width - 70 inches/ transom height - 24 inches/ maximum hull depth - 34 inches/ approximate weight - 2000 pounds.

"The Havasu"
17 FOOT OUTBOARD

"The Finest In Family Outboards"

This family fun boat comes equipped with two back-to - back vinyl seats/ indoor - outdoor carpet/ storage compartment for fuel tank and battery/ Mark II Steermaster controls.

Specifications: Lenght - 16 feet 2 inches/ beam - 78 inches transon width - 64 inches/ transon height - 21 inches approximate weight - 750 pounds.

SPECIFICATIONS:

THE TAHOE CRUISER

Length 21 feet / Beam 93" / Transom width 84" / Transom height 30" / Maximum hull depth 34" / Approximate weight 2500 lbs. / Carpeting / Beautiful wood-grained side storage panels cover roomy ski and storage areas / General vinyl all-weather seating / Choice of solid colors (or twenty metalflake combinations at slight additional cost).

PROPULSION POWER & INSTRUMENTS:
Standard equipment: Ford-Lincoln marine engine, 460 cubic inch / 12 volt solid state alternator with built-in regulator / Heavy duty battery / Bilge pump / Bilge exhaust blower / Keyed ignition switch / Tachometer, alternator output, oil pressure and water temperature gauges / Berkeley Jet-Drive standard unit / Morse single level throttle and shift control / with optional color steering wheel / Engines optional 340hp, 405hp, 450hp all 454 cubic inch Chevrolet.

CONSTRUCTION:
Polyester reinforced fiberglass outer hull with laminations up to one inch thick. Two vertical grain select Douglas Fir stringers cut from choice 2" by 6" lumber. Each Tahoe Cruiser is custom crafted by hand laid-up material.

STANDARD AND OPTIONAL ITEMS:
Standard equipment includes two built-in fuel boat tanks / passenger assist grip / engine cover / safety support / Standard Seating for 8 people color to match / ski-tow.

Optional equipment available, stainless steel impeller / metalflake color combinations / deck hardware / bow and stern lights / cigarette lighter / windshield / swim step / bow rail / and a large variety of marine accessories.

This boat was made in 1973 for John Robinson and was shipped to Australia. It was made exactly like Coldfire except the yellow flames were changed to white.

In November 1980, the Australian Boating Federation, who had been reading about Julian Pettengill in magazines, called and asked Julian if he would come to Australia to race. Julian raced this flatbottom against three unlimited hydroplanes on a 2½ mile course with an island in the middle. He was ahead the whole race until one of them cut him off 30 feet from the finish line and Julian came in second.

This boat was an exact copy of Coldfire, so these pictures show what Coldfire looked like.

The foot pedal system had three pedals that Julian used to control the altitude of the boat. The first pedal was the throttle. He would push on the second pedal to raise the front of the boat for the straightaway. When he came to a corner, he would push the third pedal and it would drop the nose really hard on the fins so he could turn the boat very sharp and quick. Julian always said that if he could go into and out of the corners 5 mph faster than any other boat, he could just about win any race. The other drivers accused him of cutting them off in the turns, but it was actually just hard driving.

Arizona Ski Boats 1974

We were still building Biesemeyer Boats at the shop on 59th Avenue. Julian Pettengill was continuing to win races in the Biesemeyer Boat named Coldfire. He won the Easter Divisionals that year, but he didn't run in the National Championships because of Gordon Jennings' death.

During the first part of 1974, I got burned out working on boats. I went to work building cabinets for Dave Jackson, who owned Jackson Cabinets. He and I had the same hobby of remote-control airplanes.

Julian Pettengill and Paul Edwards owned and ran Arizona Ski Boats. There were no longer any Biesemeyers in the business.

Conrad Murphy

Rusty had a shop on 35th Avenue, where he cut down a K-boat so it would fit in the E-boat class. He built it for Conrad Murphy who went on set the kilo record for E-boats at a little over 112 mph. Conrad Murphy never won a circle race.

In 1974, Julian set a new kilo record in Coldfire with a speed of 127.85 mph. A kilo race is a straightaway race of a little over a half mile. They race twice, once in each direction and the average of both runs is the kilo time.

Driving Coldfire, Julian Pettengill won the Regatta of Champions at Marine Stadium in Long Beach, California in 1974.

This Biesemeyer Boat, built in 1974, was originally silver and was sold to a doctor back east. The doctor traded it for another boat and this one was eventually sold to Wayne Herbert who had it painted exactly like Coldfire, with the same number, K-50. He entered it in many boat shows and it won every time.

Herbert had Dave Bryant drive it at Nationals in August of 2009 and it won. It was 35 years old at the time it won Nationals.

Arizona Ski Boats 1975

Julian Pettengill and Paul Edwards were still making Biesemeyer Boats and Julian won the Nationals that year in Coldfire.

These pictures from the June 1975 issue of *Race Boat and Industry News* show some of the Biesemeyer Boats that were winning races in 1975.

COLD FIRE — There was no doubt about it - Julian Pettengill and his sleek green Bubby Wilton powered Biesemeyer were at their finest, winning both heats through rough water, and slinging around the corners like a railroad locomotive.

ANGEL FIRE - Julian Pettengill, seemingly unbeatable in Paul Edwards sharp Biesemeyer, did it again this weekend, averaging over three miles per hour faster than his nearest rival, winning both heats.

HONCHO - John Peters super-consistent Biesemeyer, driven by Jarrol Jamison, picked up another second place trophy, finishing there both heats, a fair distance ahead of its nearest competition.

NEVER ENUFF - Gil Suiter's new Hallett by Barron was shoed capably by Danny Mang, who managed a second place in the Superstock class. The boat is loaded with potential.

NEVER ENUFF - Gil Suiter's sharp Hallett by Barron, driven by Danny Mang, was super-impressive enroute victory in the 454-cubic inch and under class, in defeating second place Mike Scott of Scottsdale, Ariz.

LIGHT MY FIRE - Second behind Clune, with a pair of seconds, was Stan Morrish's sharp Chevy powered Biesemeyer.

PRIDE - Julian Pettengill drove the Beisemeyer to victory in the competitive Superstock class, which like nearly all runabout classes, ran only one heat.

Biesemeyer

BY ARIZONA SKI BOATS
Home of "Cold Fire" K50, World's fastest Circle K-boat.

THE NAME AND BOAT THAT SPEAKS FOR ITSELF... JUST CHECK THE RECORDS.

The king of the K class, Julian Pettengill in "Cold Fire", 1971 National Champ, 1973 National Champ, 1973 US1, 1973 High Points, UIM World record holder at 102.81 average speed for 5 miles.

This performance cruiser is designed roomily to give your family and friends the ultimate in comfort and performance, with responsive acceleration, fast planing and a velvet smooth ride.

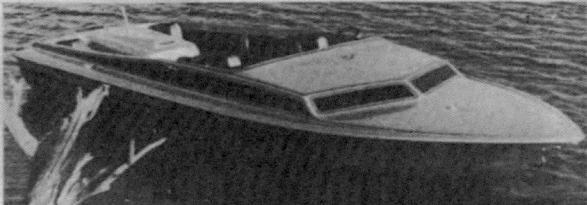
A one-of-its-kind styling; check out its sleek lines, length of its deck and room for family comfort.

Brent Berge's SS88 "Pride"

Mel Friend's "Thumper Pumper"

QUALITY AND PERFORMANCE
18 FOOT JET • 18 FOOT FLATBOTTOM • 21 FOOT DAY CRUISER

ARIZONA SKI BOATS
414 SOUTH 59TH AVE. • PHOENIX, ARIZONA 85009 • (602) 278-8044

Julian Pettengill had new deck molds made for the K-boat because he wanted the dashboard moved forward so his legs wouldn't get caught under it in a crash.

Bubby Wilton was a great engine builder and he built all of Julian's supercharged engines. This was the cover picture on the June 1975 issue of *Race Boat and Industry News*. Julian is on the left and Bubby is on the right.

JULIAN PETTENGILL: MENACE OR MASTER?
Race Boat and Industry News - June 1975

"He's a poor, crude, reckless driver. He'll run over or through anything to win. He will do anything to win." - a top K class driver, talking about Julian Pettengill, driver of the Biesemeyer K boat COLDFIRE, SK craft ANGELFIRE, and SS racer PRIDE.

"I've never hit anybody. I've never hurt anyone. But the object of racing is not second place. The second place guy's a loser. There's only one winner - in anything." - Julian Pettengill, talking about himself.

Julian Keenan Pettengill, 38 years old, entered into the addicting sport of circle boat racing in 1968 - ironically, as a fun-type venture, driving a green flatbottom with a ski tow poking obtrusively toward the dry Arizona skyline which hovers over the place Julian calls home.

Seven years later, a point in time which Pettengill swears through uncannily deep blue eyes that this will be his final competitive season, Pettengill can truly say he has done it all. And now, it's more than simple fun. Pettengill's the most serious, business-like driver on the course.

Between the beginning, and what he adamantly insists will be the end; between the first APBA Nationals win at Seattle, Washington, and the last win at Long Beach, the compact, often-smiling owner of Arizona Ski Boats has garnered his share of wins, more than his share of criticism, and indisputably more than anyone's share of notoriety.

He has been hated by his competition, perhaps more so than anyone ever. That feeling was perhaps best exemplified in the heat of last season's racing action, when certain members of the K Racing Runabout class circulated a volatile petition, which strongly suggested banning Pettengill from racing, and more than suggested that he was a "menace."

But on the reverse side of the spectrum, Pettengill has enjoyed a love-affair with the huge following of his boat, so intense that it may never be matched.

WINNING CREW - Allen DeMore, one of the main ingredients of the winning team's formula (far left), along with Pettengill (with cigar), Miss California, and engine-builder Bubby Wilton, all leaning on ANGEL FIRE, the SK rig which debuted that weekend.

People go to the races just to see Pettengill maneuver the Bubby Wilton powered COLDFIRE through the turns and down the chutes like nobody else can.

Like one SK driver said, "Julian's forgotten more about driving than we'll ever learn."

It's a joy to watch Pettengill drive any boat - be it Allen DeMore and Paul Edwards'

ANGELFIRE, Brent Berge's PRIDE, or whatever. But Pettengill and COLDFIRE go together like scotch and water.

Julian Pettengill, talking about other drivers' attitudes about him: "It used to bother me. I used to get so damn mad I was ready to punch their lights out. But now, I've learned to take it with a grain of salt. In fact, I probably would have gotten out of it by now, but they've antagonized me to the degree where I have a point to prove."

Julian Pettengill, talking about spectators and the magnetism which exists around COLDFIRE: "The spectators don't know me from Adam. That's just the way I like it. They know the boat, and that's it. Sometimes I like to get away from the pits during the races, and watch the show alone. I go to the bleachers, get away from all the garbage."

Don't get the idea that every one in racing is out to get Pettengill. Superlatives like "the best," "super," and "spectacular" seem to flow easily from the mouth of many of Pettengill's racing counterparts.

But Julian is purely and simply one of those people that don't blend in with the crowd. Either you like him immensely, or you can't stand him. And conversely, if he doesn't particularly care for you, you'll know it.

"I try to be honest with people." Pettengill said. "I'll never say anything behind someone's back that I won't say to their faces. That's one major thing I have against a lot of people who put me down when I'm on the race course."

Pettengill's fiery driving career, which has spanned three different COLDFIRE hulls, actually began at Pleasant Lake, Arizona, a resort a short distance from Phoenix. He began competing under the auspices of the Arizona Navy, a local Phoenix boat and ski club that's been around since 1930 - longer than any of it's fellow APBA rivals. In his first race, Pettengill went into a turn, and was welcomed to boat racing by a wayward competitor charging across Julian's deck, tearing it to pieces.

For the next three years, Pettengill dabbled in racing. But it wasn't really a serious thing with him. Winning has always been important - but it wasn't an obsession at that time.

Things changed drastically in 1971, when COLDFIRE hit the big time. It was at one of Pettengill's first APBA races - the Nationals at Seattle, Washington.

"I wasn't all jacked up about the race," Julian recalled. "I figured a third or a fourth would be great. I was running a boat that we had skied behind for three years. On the first day of qualifying, I won my heat, and went over the record."

Julian averaged over 90 miles per hour that day. But his chances for victory on Sunday seemed as slim as the needle nosed bow of the metal-flaked green Biesemeyer he was driving.

COLD FIRE - Julian Pettengill has been called a menace by some - but he's proven he's a master, at the wheel of the Bubby Wilton owned and powered Biesemeyer Unlimited circle boat, always a front-runner.

ANGEL FIRE - Pettengill has also been a dominating factor in the beautiful SK entry he has become so adept at throttling.

"We were running a sick horse," Julian laughed, remembering the shape of his engine. "It was worn out before we brought it up there, and we knew it."

After a patch job in John Gurrison's Seattle shop, Pettengill jockeyed his "sick horse" to first place the next day. The name COLDFIRE, which was derived through the boat-builder's color chart (which tagged the boat's silver-green color "cold fire" at that time) was rapidly shot through the wide-open grapevine of boat-racing's following. But that was only the beginning.

As Pettengill's success snowballed, he became increasingly more serious. And more sensitive. The sensitivity was kindled by official rulings which seemed, at least in Pettengill's eyes, to always go against him.

Like the time in San Diego when Julian's water-line broke on the first lap of his heat. He pulled into the infield, removed his helmet so he could fit his head between the seat, the boat, and the header for examination of the engine. His helmet was off for 15 seconds according to APBA officials' time.

When Julian returned to the beach, he was notified of the official ruling handed down - he was disqualified from this race and his drivers license was revoked for a period of six months.

"That's the only time that's ever happened to anybody." Pettengill said, of the suspension. "I can show you photos of ten different drivers doing the same thing, with nothing ever happening to them. I felt it was a little stiff."

Thus began a hate-affair between Julian and San Diego, which seems to become increasingly heated with each event there. Since the helmet incident, Julian says, he has been the butt of offbeat rulings and political decisions.

Just last month (the April San Diego circle meet) he was disqualified for gun-jumping in the SK class. When he asked to see the photo of the start, which is taken as each race begins to determine premature starters, he was confronted by a sheepish official.

"You won't believe this," the official said. "But the photo of your start is the only one all day that didn't print."

Pettengill started to say something to the effect of the official being right about his credibility rating, when he was interrupted by another official.

"One of their big-shots jumped up and said that if I said another word, he would beach me for the year." Pettengill said. "I almost jumped up and let it fly, but I didn't. I've exploded too many times, and it's just not worth it. Those people don't realize that I can do without them."

If Pettengill's reputation seems shaky in some parts, his actual credentials are as solid as the masterful blown Bubby Wilton motor that has driven him to win after win after win.

Flanking his cluttered Arizona Ski Boats office desk are a pair of gleaming wall-plaques, signifying APBA National Championships in 1971 and 1973 (the helmet suspension kept him from competing in 1972, and Pettengill refused to run in Utah in 1974 because of K racer Gordon Jennings' death.

A certificate, proclaiming Pettengill an official U.I.M. world record-holder at 102.86 miles per hour, in the 5-mile competition category, also hangs on the wall, as do a dozen or more photos of COLDFIRE and ANGELFIRE in various shapes and angles - including upside down.

Pettengill doesn't know how many trophies he has collected, but excluding the ones awarded Wilton and crew, he says the number probably stands around 60 or so.

But through all the statistics, past all the photos of the boats in circular motion, through all the plaques, something which is obviously of equal or greater importance to Julian shines through. People.

"Winning isn't luck," said Pettengill. "It takes the right people. I've got them."

For a time, Pettengill did his own wrenching. It was while racing that Julian became associated with Leon "Bubby" Wilton - a man whose own attitude of "win at any cost" is said to be rivaled only by Julian Keenan Pettengill's.

Wilton was running COLD TURKEY, a moderately successful K boat. A standing joke between Wilton and Pettengill, at that time, was "if we only used your boat, and my motor . . ."

That joke was transformed into iron reality one early morning of November, 1972, when the upcoming Parker kilo races found Pettengill with a lame motor, and lack of time or funds to get his motor in first-class shape. A team was born - over the phone.

Pettengill drove to Wilton's Los Angeles shop the Wednesday night before the weekend races, and the motor was planted Thursday. It was back to Arizona for the kilos, where Pettengill was anxious, yet a bit reluctant, to savor his first taste of supercharged power.

"I had never driven a blown boat before that weekend," he recalled. "I made about five practice passes, and was having a hell of a time. I was convinced there was no way I could do it."

Pettengill was about to put the green machine on the trailer, unconquered, when the "what the hell" attitude took over. One more time Pettengill nailed his foot to the fiberglass floor - and this time it stayed there.

"I was going to do it - whether or not I ended up on my head," Julian laughed.

PRIDE - Pettengill, who will run all three classes at the Nationals this year, has also taken his share of Superstock trophies.

The result of that very run was an astounding 125 mile per hour plus pass, with a 126 plus on the down-the river run - for a new kilo record of 125.80 miles per hour.

The next day, Gordon Jennings of San Diego, California, popped a surprising down-river run of over 137 miles per hour, tilting his average to 126.153 miles per hour - a new kilo record, shattering Pettengill's one-day old mark. Julian came back to better that mark - at 127.746 miles per hour the same day - but it didn't exceed the necessary record-breaking requirement of one per cent.

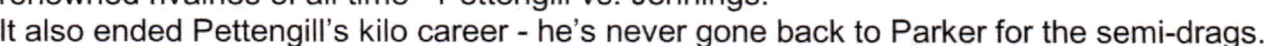
K-50 - The famed COLD FIRE numerals.

That kilo event sparked one of the most renowned rivalries of all time - Pettengill vs. Jennings. It also ended Pettengill's kilo career - he's never gone back to Parker for the semi-drags.

The Pettengill-Jennings thing, a vicious competition that was one mighty factor of the K classes' magnanimous growth over the past three years, was not what many people liked to believe.

"Gordy was a great guy, and a great driver. We really got along well," Julian said.

It was no coincidence that when Jennings took his fatal crash at the Provo, Utah K Nationals, that Pettengill was the first to reach Gordon to the water - the first to discover that it was too late.

It was also no accident that Pettengill put his boat on the trailer as soon as Jennings was taken from the course, refusing to compete any more in that event. And no mere coincidence that Pettengill voted (in vain) to cancel further K national competition that year, and name Jennings Honorary National Champion.

"It wouldn't have been an honor to win. It wasn't even an honor to race. I couldn't have raced after that," Pettengill said.

Somehow the "poor, reckless driver. . . will do anything to win," description about Julian quoted earlier fails to flush here.

Pettengill, Wilton, DeMore, are parts of the fantastic success story. Joining them are Paul Edwards, Pettengill's faithful companion and business partner, another key to the operation. It's obvious that Edwards, quick to defend Julian's driving tactics, feels there's only one leader of the circle pack. Jack Lee, Jimmy Anderson, Barry Ross - these individuals are also key members of the Pettengill racing entourage.

Julian Pettengill was walking through the dusty, desert land on which his boat-building facilities are constructed. He sauntered to a spot near the side of his building, where two dilapidated, old torn green hulls lay - remains of day gone by. The "National Champion" insignias, inscribed on both decks, were faded by days of erosion supplied by the merciless Phoenix sun and wind. Pettengill looked fondly at the two former members of the COLDFIRE tradition, and wiped his finger through a thick layer of dirt and grime covering one of the metal-flaked green craft.

"I'm going to miss it all when I'm gone," he said, mostly to himself.

And when he's gone, they're going to miss Julian. Some will be happy about it. Most will not. But everyone will know Julian's not there. He's just that kind of a guy.

1976

Julian Pettengill's races and championships

COLDFIRE K-50 (K Racing Runabouts)

    1971
    National Champion

    1972
    Kilo Record 127.850
    Regatta of Champions

    1973
    High Point U.S. 1
    Regatta of Champions
    5 Mile Competition World Record Holder 102.857 mph
    National Champion

    1974
    Eastern Divisionals Champion

    1975
    National Champion

    1976
    Summer Nationals Champion
    Winter Nationals Champion
    Regatta of Champions
    Boating Hall of Fame

ANGELFIRE SK-295 (Pro Comp)

    1976
    Winter Nationals West Champion

NEVER ENUFF SS-1 (Super Stock)

    1975
    Winter Nationals West Champion

    1976
    Summer Nationals West Champion
    Summer Nationals East Champion
    5 Mile Competition Record Holder 94.142 mph
    Canadian Boating Federation Record Holder

Alan Demore bought 4 or 5 Biesemeyer Boats from Rusty through the years. This one was Angelfire.

Bubby Wilton, pictured above, built most of the engines for the boats Julian drove. Bubby's engines were so good that Julian never had to worry about an engine breaking while he was racing.

This Biesemeyer Boat was called Never Enuff. It was a boat owned by Gil Suiter and driven by Julian Pettengill. In 1975 it won the Winter Nationals West. In 1976, it won the Summer Nationals West, the Summer Nationals East, and was the Canadian Boating Federation record holder. It was also the record holder in a five-mile competition at 94.142 mph.

If you won a national race, you could put a sticker on your boat with a "1" on it. Since he won so many races in his class, he had a "1" painted permanently on Never Enuff.

The SS on the side of the boat stands for Super Stock. Super Stock Runabouts must run American-made stock passenger car engines and may not exceed 428 cubic inches. They must run on gasoline or aviation fuel with a maximum of four venturis. With very limited exceptions, engines must be stock as manufactured. Cavitation plates are permitted and may be adjusted while the boat is under way. Hull specifications are the same as applied to all other flatbottom classes.

This is Alan Demore's Biesemeyer Boat, "Angelfire. It was an SK class number 295 that Julian Pettengill drove when he won the Winter Nationals West in 1976.

SK stands for ski boat. The SK Runabouts must run American-made automotive engines and may not exceed 400 cubic inches. They must have carburetors, not fuel injection, and they must run on gasoline. All internal and external engine modifications and ignition systems are accepted.

JULIAN PETTENGILL

Circle-boat-driver extraordinaire

A number of extremely talented drivers have filtered through the K Racing Runabout (KRR) ranks, which pits a track full of 18- to 20-foot blown fuel flatbottoms in hairy, closed-course action, but in the early-1970s, Julian Pettengill dominated it like no one before or since.

The K boat is the ultimate circle-track boat, mixing alcohol and full-on blower motors with 18- to 20-foot flatbottoms—essentially releasing a fleet of V-drive dragsters into intermittent hairpin turns and 125-mph straightaways. Pettengill won the K Nationals three times, averaged a record-shattering 102.857 miles an hour through five miles of competition, was US#1 in pints in 1973 and set a kilo record of 127.850 mph in 1972. In a field of the most talented drivers in circle racing, Pettengill was nearly unbeatable and universally revered, and the APBA inducted him into its Hall of Fame in 1976.

Remarkably, Pettengill routinely climbed from his K boat into a carbureted SK racer and then into a Pro Comp flatbottom—competing in three circle-racing classes in a weekend. He was a dual-class record holder, owning the Pro Comp five-mile competition mark at 94.12 mph, and won several National event titles.

He was known as a fiery competitor who would not back down, on the water or off, and drove the course like he owned it and was often accused of being over-aggressive. "It's like anything," says Pettengill, reflecting on his hard-edged reputation. "If you win a few of 'em in a row, nobody likes you."

At times, he made that easy. He towed to Miami for the Nationals in 1971, won them and was disqualified after his hull was proclaimed illegal by APBA officials. Pettengill hired an attorney and sued—and came away with his title and a mandated letter of apology from APBA. Pettengill promptly took out an ad and published that letter in the predecessor to HOT BOAT, the tabloid Race Boat and Industry News.

He was later kicked out of APBA for six months for removing his helmet on the race course after an event. "Me and APBA had a rocky road of it," said Pettengill in a recent telephone interview. The key to his success? "I had some good people around me," Pettengill declared, correctly deferring proper credit to legendary engine builder Bubby Wilton and a devoted support cast.

Julian Pettingill and Coldfire

Coldfire was a K-Boat. K Racing Runabouts are unrestricted as to the use of engines. There is no displacement limit or price limit. Fuel and superchargers are allowed to be used, which makes this class the fastest of all inboard circle boats. The hulls must conform to general inboard runabout rules and may use cavitation plates that can be adjusted while the boat is underway. Each new K driver must participate in a minimum of three heats, starting behind the pack, to insure the driver is capable of driving this class of boat.

In some race events, Julian drove four boats, Coldfire, Anglefire, Never Enuff, and Rascal, a Pro Comp boat.

Jamie Jamison was a teenage kid who hung around the Biesemeyer Boat shops. He was a master at striping boats. He later went on to paint whole boats and was the best custom painter around. He painted most of Julian's boats and many more Biesemeyer Boats. Jamie became a very good boat driver, driving his pro-comp class Biesemeyer Boat. There was an article in *Hot Boat Magazine* about him in March 1986. Here are some excerpts from the article:

"Jamie's success on the water has filled his den with plenty of gold hardware. He went undefeated in four seasons before losing at the APBA Nationals. He has captured numerous memorial honors from Southern California Speedboat Association. Last season he finally won the Nationals in addition to earning national high-points. Twice he was named driver of the year by the Marine Academy Awards. Early this year, Jamie was inducted into the APBA Hall of Champions, joining 172 others. One year at Canyon Lake, Jamison won a Hot Boat money race, prompting John Peters to offer, 'I'll build a race boat if you drive it.' The team's first outing proved to be about their best in the K-class. In 1974 in Seattle, Jamison finished second to the legendary Julian Pettengill. From there they scored limited success. In 1976, just as they were getting the boat properly dialed in, the engine seized during the race at Firebird, sending the nose into the water. Jamie went back to driving pro-comp."

As of 2009, Jamie still had a paint shop that did custom painting on boats and cars.

Jamie Jamison

1977-1978

Julian Pettengill was inducted into the American Power Boat Association's Hall of Champions and was honored for the inboard category.

The June 1978 issue of Custom Boat & Engine ran an article titled *APBA Hall of Champions Honors Julian Pettengill*. It said in part:

"Colorful, competitive, controversial – circle boat driver Julian Pettengill has shown that he is all of this . . . and much more. Induction into the American Power Boat Association's Hall of Champions is the most recent acknowledgment of his achievements in a remarkable racing career.

"This year Julian Pettengill was honored for the inboard category. Julian first started his racing career in the early 1960s when he used to ski race for fun. His first A.P.B.A. race wasn't until 1970 when he started driving his own K Racing Runabout, K-50 Coldfire. 'Then the K's were more or less like the Pro Comps are now. I remember the Super Stocks going out and beating us,' says Julian. 'The K's weren't blown and we didn't have the driver qualifications as we do now.'

"Julian's first major win and one of his favorites, was the 1971 A.P.B.A. Nationals in his K.R.R. It was the third competitive race he had ever entered.

"Julian races approximately 40 weekends in one racing season. This includes all Nationals and Divisionals wherever they may be in the United States.

"Does Julian Pettengill have any specific goals for the future? That's a tough question, since he has already accomplished just about everything a boat racer can ask for . . and then some. 'I like to race and I like the people involved with racing. I have fun whether I'm driving or just spending the day spectating.'"

BOAT RACER STILL GAME, DESPITE NEAR-FATAL CRASH
The Phoenix Gazette - April 28, 1977

If you would compute Julian Pettengill's chances of winning the American Power Boat Association Western Championship at Firebird Lake this weekend, you'd have ro rate them pretty good.

Pettengill has won 100 of 103 heats he ran last year.

"Once, while I was in second place trying to get into first place, my boat turned upside down," declared the Phoenix racer, grinning. "It happened at Long Beach Marine Stadium in July 1975.

"I guess I was giving it too much gas when I turned the corner, and the boat flipped out at 110 miles per hour. My parachute – we use one for deceleration – got tangled in the wreckage.

"Everything sunk and I sunk with it."

Pettengill was underwater four minutes. It felt like four hours to the victim and the people on shore who took desperate life-saving actions to get him out.

After several hours in the emergency room at a local hospital, he was sent home, feeling lucky to be alive.

"They hadn't gotten all the water out of my lungs," he added. "I woke up the next morning feeling terrible and had to be rushed to the hospital emergency room at Temple City. I spent a month on crutches."

Pettengill, who owns Arizona Ski Boats at 414 S. 59th Ave., will be competing with boat racers from throughout the country for $19,000 in prize money.

Pettengill, who flies a private plane, has operated drag cars but says nothing compares with a 1,500-HP racing boat for speed.

"A boat traveling 100 miles per hour compares to a car going 200," he insisted. "There's much more sensation of speed in a boat. For one thing, the ground doesn't move on a car. You've got to read the water correctly or you're in bad trouble."

There are many differences between the average pleasure boat and a racing boat. The pleasure boat will have less than 100 HP while its racing counterpart often has up to 1,500 HP in a hull weighing no more than 500 pounds.

Racing boats can hit over 150 miles per hour on the straightaways. On a good day with a still wind helping, a pleasure boat might reach 40.

The price is different, too. Pleasure boats are sold for around $6,000 each, while a racing boat is painstakingly built by hand, with costs reaching up to $20,000.

"That's why I run boats for other people," said Pettengill. "It just costs too much to do it by yourself."

Ending of Arizona Ski Boats 1981

Julian Pettengill and Arizona Ski Boats continued to build Biesemeyer Boats until 1981. About 1980, the economy was down, and boat sales dropped due to government regulations taking control of the boat industry.

Julian sold the boat molds to Norm Brown in Lake Havasu City, Arizona. He then started an air-conditioning company in the same shop making a special kind of cooler. Later he sold this business to Sam Walton of Walmart.

The January 1991 issue of *National Circle Boat Magazine* wrote an article titled "25 All Time Greatest Powerboat Drivers" which said:

"18. Julian Pettengill drove 'Coldfire' a 'K-Boat' that I never saw beaten. I saw the accident that destroyed the hull but Julian came right back to win numerous SS and K races. Julian would make those flat bottoms just quiver going down the straight-a-ways. To watch him drive was like watching MAGIC."

After Biesemeyer Boats

Rusty Biesemeyer died in 1984. Four years later, in 1988, the Arizona Navy, a Phoenix boat club, started a memorial race called the Rusty Biesemeyer Regatta. The race ran annually from 1988 until 1992. All of the boats that raced in the flatbottom classes at the Regatta were Biesemeyer Boats or a direct copy.

Rusty Biesemeyer 1978

Today, all of the Biesemeyer Boats and installations are the same as they were 30 years ago when Rusty and Julian designed them. The boat that continue to win are Biesemeyer Boats or a copy. The last Biesemeyer Boat to win a championship was owned by Wayne Herbert and driven by Dave Bryant. It was 35 years old and won the Nationals in 2009 at Long Beach, California.

HALLETT'S NEW 260 AC
PLUS! POWERQUEST'S HOT 380

Hot Boat
THE ONLY PERFORMANCE BOATING MAGAZINE THAT MATTERS

www.hotboat.net

WALK-THROUGH WONDERS!
We Test 8 Family Bowriders
SEE PAGE 42

POWERQUEST'S 380

HOT BOAT HALL OF FAME
5 Industry Legends Inducted

PLUS:
- 16-Page Custom Section
- TOPPS Poker Run
- Bay City River Roar

SEPTEMBER 2003
$4.99/$6.99 Canada

2003 HOT BOAT HALL OF FAME

RUSTY BIESEMEYER

MASTER HULL DESIGNER

He showed a natural design talent from the beginning: The first boat he built, a nine-foot three-point hydro, won the Outboard National Championships in 1953.

Talk about new technology all you want, but in the full-contact world of circle-boat racing, where handling counts for everything, Rusty Biesemeyer's flatbottom design still lives large nearly 20 years after his death. Absolutely dominating in K-boat racing and Superstock when he released it in 1970, the double-straked Biesemeyer Sprint boat remains, in its various permutations, the go-to hull for today's serious flatbottom racer.

Famous for its ability to carve hard in the turns and unleash blistering, natural speed in the straights, the Sprint held every competition K-boat and SK record worth holding at various times. The most dominant K-racer in history, *Cold Fire*, was perhaps the most famous in a heap of championship-caliber Biesemeyers.

But the Sprint boat was only one of more than 15 groundbreaking hulls designed and produced at Biesemeyer's Phoenix-based boat shop, a prolific haven of creative thinking that overflowed into drag and circle racing, as well as the production ranks.

Famous for its hard carving ability and blistering natural speed, the Sprint held every competition record worth holding and won countless races and innumerable championships, beneath the likes of Julian Pettengill, among others. It was one of more than 15 hulls designed and produced by Biesemeyer.

It is this natural acumen for design, backed by a supreme level of commitment and ingenuity that propelled Rusty Biesemeyer into the HOT BOAT Hall of Fame, where he assumes residence among the other master hull designers of his day.

Biesemeyer's prolific imagination and savvy, seat-of-the-pants engineering was not contained to the racecourse. He was a trailblazer in early production of fiberglass performance boats and designed and built one of the first Day Cruisers—if not the first. And his Caribbean ski boat, tooled in 1960, set new styling standards that were quickly emulated, and their appeal has proven immune to the test of time.

Of course, there was constant crossover between the pleasure- and race-boating realms.

After his brother introduced Rusty to boats in 1953, his vocation of exotic cars took a turn toward the water. He showed a natural design talent from the beginning: The first boat he built, a nine-foot three-point hydro, won the Outboard National Championships in 1953. His natural inclination was to add power, and that led to the creation of an all-wood Ski Racer in 1954, which was rigged up with a Studebaker off a hydraulic clutch.

In 1956, Biesemeyer released one of the first, if not the first, all-fiberglass production inboard, a 16-footer—reportedly the first tooling to be mocked and molded with compound curves. An offshoot design that capitulated into a modified, "double bubble" four-point hydro—powered by a stock, 358 Chevy—was the first boat to run 125 miles an hour in the quarter mile, at Long Beach Marine Stadium, in 1959—beating Mickey Thompson in the final round. One of the early, dominant race boats of the day, the *Pied Piper* was owned by Jaque Pettijohn. A series of milestones would follow in the Biesemeyer's wake.

Biesemeyer was forever experimenting, breaking new ground. In 1967, he built a flatbottom with strakes on the bottom. Two years later, the 21-foot Day Cruiser emerged. In 1970, the Sprint hull instantly accelerated peak speeds in the serious racing ranks, and, in 1974, the Murphy-Biesemeyer 17-footer emerged and instantly became the world's fastest unblown gas flatbottom.

Biesemeyer would eventually sell his molds to Julian Pettengill, who successfully produced the 18-foot Biesemeyer for a number of years.

Editor's note: Special thanks to Conrad Murphy for his assistance in preparing this story.

Rusty Biesemeyer Regatta

$1.00

February 6-7, 1988
Phoenix, Arizona

AMERICAN POWER BOAT ASSOCIATION

RUSTY BIESEMEYER

Rusty Biesemeyer was obsessed. For thousands of grateful boating enthusiasts, this obsession and his vision have provided years of thrilling boating experiences.

The Biesemeyer era of boat design was launched in 1956. Rusty was introduced to boat manufacturing when his brother Bill built several wooden boats. Rusty was hooked!

Throughout his 28 year boating history, Rusty had a string of "firsts" and boating records that were nothing short of incredible. First and foremost, he was unrelenting in his quest to continually improve the ski boat design. He built the first all-fiberglass hulls for big engines. He designed and built one of the first 20 foot jet powered day cruisers. The 14 and 16 foot outboards he designed and built were, like the others, terrific performers.

In 1961, Rusty built what many considered to be his most beautiful design . . . the Caribbean hull. However, the ultimate in the Rusty Biesemeyer legacy of boat designs are the K Class Flat Bottom Hulls. These are still successful in winning races today. Hulls designed by Rusty have won many races and broken many records. Typical of these is the very successful Murphy-Biesemeyer E Boat.

Rusty's career in boat design successfully spanned the period from 1956 until his death in 1984. But, today, Rusty continues to give us a lot of thrills and a lot of satisfaction.

Rusty Biesemeyer . . . Thank you!

RUSTY BIESEMEYER AT THE 1957 PHOENIX BOAT SHOW

1991 INBOARD WESTERN DIVISIONALS

4th Annual Rusty Biesemeyer Regatta

May 4-5, 1991
Phoenix, Arizona

AMERICAN POWER BOAT ASSOCIATION

$1.00

"RUSTY ABOUT TO TEST THE FIRST BIESEMEYER DAYCRUISER"

Visit The Manufacturers Display Area
Located Behind The Grandstand

Biesemeyer BOATS
A truly new concept in boating

"You Couldn't Find a Better Boat for the Motor of Your Choice"

14 ft. Outboard... $895./16 ft. Outboard... $1195

ADVERTISEMENT IN OCTOBER 1959 WEST COAST BOATING NEWSPAPER.
$895.00 FOR A 14' RUNABOUT — NOT BAD, HUH?

K RACING RUNABOUTS

K RACING RUNABOUTS are unrestricted as to the use of engines. There is no displacement limit or price limit. Fuel and superchargers are allowed to be used, which makes this class the fastest of all inboard circle boats. The hulls must conform to general inboard runabout rules and may use cavitation plates that can be adjusted while the boat is underway. Each new K driver must participate in a minimum of three heats, strting behind the pack. This is done to insure the driver is capable of driving in this class of boat. Straightaway speeds up to 140 MPH.

BOAT NO. AND NAME		OWNER AND DRIVER, CITY AND STATE	HULL	ENGINE
Kilometer Record: 146-649				
	Freedom	Richard Thompson, Anaheim, CA Gordon Jennings, Jr., Anaheim, CA	Biesemeyer	Chevrolet
5 Mile Circle Record (4 Laps): 104.950				
	Freedom	Richard Thompson, Anaheim, CA Gordon Jennings, Jr., Anaheim, CA	Biesemeyer	Chevrolet
K9	Kelron Racing Special	Ronald Bolton, Long Beach, CA	Spitfire	Chevrolet
K17	Hangman	Larry Dahlhoff, Norco, CA		
K90	Dark Side of The Moon	Bill Moore, Anaheim, CA Marty Ceccarelli, Phoenix, AZ	Revenge	Chevrolet
K7	Krazy Kanuk	Guy Verdon, Sorel, Quebec, Canada	Revenge	Chevrolet
K69	Freedom	Richard Thompson, Anaheim, CA Gordon Jennings, Jr., Anaheim, CA	Biesemeyer	Chevrolet
K6	Valve Train Special	Val Wheeler, Anaheim, CA Bill Pagett, La Habra, CA	D'Cucci	Chevrolet
K13	Kaos	Clyde Morgan, Irvine, CA		
K214		Ronald Sporl, Metairie, LA		
K14	Hobbit	Charles Boyd, Victorville, CA George Stratton, Rialto, CA	Daytona	Chevrolet
K525	Sinister Purpose	Bernie O'Niel, Long Beach, CA Jim Patchett, Torrence, CA		
K777	War Eagle	Phil Stock, Orange, CA Bob Bode, Barrington, IL	Revenge	Chevrolet
K16	Shocker	John Gutherie, Cerritos, CA		
K21	Black Jack	Roger Glover, Reno, NV	Capsule	Boat
K75		Junior Hart, West Jordan, UT		
K555		Dave Rankin, Whittier, CA		
K98	Mickeys Revenge	Darrell Dockery, Phoenix, AZ		
K390	Distant Thunder	Samma Thompson, Anaheim, CA Paul Fitzgerald, Lake Elsinore, CA	Daytona	Chevrolet

The previous page is out of the 1992 *Rusty Biesemeyer Regatta*. All of the boats with different names were made from molds taken off of Biesemeyer Boats. We think there were about ten different molds taken off of the Biesemeyer K-boat. At the boat races Julian went to 20-30 years later, most of the winners were still boats with the Biesemeyer name on them.

Julian Pettengill 1970s

Julian Pettengill about 1999

Julian Pettengill, Diane Palmer, Bill Biesemeyer - 2010

I could have never made this book without Julian's help and all of his pictures and articles. Also, this book would not have been possible without my daughter's talented computer magic.

Bill Biesemeyer - after Biesemeyer Boats

Some have asked me what I did after I left the boat business. I went to work in a cabinet shop for a while. But my bad back needed a second back operation. While I was recuperating from the surgery, I decided I was going to put the table saw fence that I had invented on the market. I called it the T-Square saw fence. I had a terrible time with it because I didn't have much money and had a small business that was really struggling.

There was a man in my church named Roger Thomson, who had been in marketing all his life. He was the right person to help me out in my little business. He borrowed some money from his brother, who was a doctor, and became a partner with 40% of the company, which we named Biesemeyer Manufacturing, Inc.

We then moved the business to Mesa, Arizona and got a larger space. Roger started taking the fence to wood working shows and the sales increased. I started inventing other tools for the cabinet shop, such as the stop system for the radial arm saw and the stop system for the miter saw. Then I invented an overhead guard for the table saw that would stay out of the way.

Powermatic started buying the T-Square table saw fence for their saws. Delta made the Delta Unisaw, but the dealers started telling Delta to ship the saw without the fence because their customers wanted the Biesemeyer T-Square fence on it.

We expanded into about eight spaces in that same building and we had about 70 employees. Delta, Powermatic, and Jet were all bidding to buy our company but Delta wanted it most so they bought it in 1995.

They eventually moved the company back to Jackson, Tennessee to the same building where they made Delta machinery and Porter Cable tools. Recently, Delta hung a 4x10-foot banner on their booth at a wood-working show to celebrate the 30th anniversary of the Biesemeyer fence and other products.

I decided to restore a 1928 Ford truck in 1987. There was a good place at the manufacturing plant to work on it and I had all the tools and equipment there that I needed. It took about four years to complete.

My hobby was making radio-controlled airplanes which I continued to do after I retired.

Bill Biesemeyer passed away August 2013. This book was put together while Bill was still alive and with his help. Countless hours were spent sitting side by side with him while he explained the pictures and related the story of Biesemeyer Boats. The book is assembled and arranged how he wanted it to be. Some editing was done and final touches were added after his death. Bill created the book for his family and wanted it published so it would be available to those who enjoy classic boats.

Diane Palmer, daughter

www.ingramcontent.com/pod-product-compliance
Lightning Source LLC
Chambersburg PA
CBRC092338290426
44108CB00009B/143